BASIC ILLUSTRATED

Map and Compass

Cliff Jacobson

FALCONGUIDES ®

GUILFORD, CONNECTICUT
HELENA, MONTANA

AN IMPRINT OF ROWMAN & LITTLEFIELD

FALCONGUIDES®

Copyright © 2008 by Cliff Jacobson

All rights reserved. No part of this book may be reproduced or transmitted in any form by any means, electronic or mechanical, including photocopying and recording, or by any information storage and retrieval system, except as may be expressly permitted by the 1976 Copyright Act or by the publisher.

Falcon and FalconGuides are registered trademarks of Rowman & Littlefield.

Text and page design by Karen Williams [intudesign.net]

Photo credits: pp. 15 top, 25, and 39 © istockphoto.com; pp. 29 top, 29 bottom, and 31 courtesy of Silva Company. All other photos are courtesy of Cliff Jacobson.
Illustration credits: pp. 8 top, 68, and 72 courtesy of U.S. Geological Survey; p. 27 top © istockphoto.com; pp. 16, 19, 21, 36, 37, 54, 55, 62, and 63 by Lon Levin; and pp. 17, 22, 39, 40, 43, 44, 45, 48 top, 48 bottom, 49, 56, 61, 69, and 70 by Cliff Moen. All other illustrations are courtesy of Cliff Jacobson.

Library of Congress Cataloging-in-Publication Data is available.

ISBN 978-0-7627-4762-7

Printed in the United States of America

Distributed by NATIONAL BOOK NETWORK

To Björn Klellstrom, whose life was shaped
by magnetism.

Contents

Preface

In 1979 the Minnesota Department of Natural Resources asked me to develop a wilderness navigation curriculum for schools and nature centers. I proposed that the prospective materials differ from existing orienteering formats by emphasizing backcountry navigation rather than competitive orienteering. Although navigational procedures are the same regardless of where you use your compass, orienteers have some real advantages over those who travel the lakes and forests.

For example, the orienteering game relies on deadly accurate large-scale maps that have magnetic declination lines drawn in. Lucky is the wilderness traveler who has such a thoughtful picture to guide the way. More often than not, outdoors people must make do with dated topographic maps or state park guides. Sure, good maps are available for just about every place in North America, but for one reason or other, few people have them. Wilderness navigation then should include the way things are as well as how they ought to be.

As I worked on the project, I discovered that outdoor enthusiasts would rather do than read, that probing complex route-finding procedures served only to confuse, while oversimplifying processes gave false confidence. And that the interpretation of contour lines—an essential component of land navigation—could, after the presentation of a few simple rules, be mastered by beginners in a matter of minutes.

Ultimately I developed a simplified approach to route finding, the rudiments of which are incorporated into this book. My own experience suggests that everything you need to know about using a map and compass is contained in these pages. If you proceed step-by-step through the chapters, you'll have no trouble finding your way in the wilderness. That's a promise.

Equipment Needed

It's pointless to begin the study of wilderness route finding without the two most important tools—a map and compass. So before you begin your study, please assemble the following materials.

1. An orienteering-style compass. No other type works as well. Indeed, you will be *severely* handicapped by any other instrument! Excellent orienteering compasses are available from the Brunton, Silva, and Suunto companies. Just type in "compasses" on any Internet search engine and you'll be deluged with choices. You'll find a thorough discussion of compasses in chapter 3.

2. Space and cost considerations prevent us from including a colored topographic practice map. Instead, we've downsized selected portions of full-size maps, pinpointing the information you need to know. While this should pose no learning difficulty, you may get the big picture more quickly if you have on hand a genuine topographic map that contains all the pieces of the puzzle on a single page.

    Any topo map will do, though, and the larger the scale, the better. A 1:24,000 (about 2.5 inches to the mile) American map or a 1:50,000 (1.25 inches equals one mile) Canadian map is ideal. Why not get a map of your favorite hunting, fishing, or hiking area? Chapter 1 tells you how to order maps.

3. An inexpensive plastic protractor is a must if you don't have an orienteering-style compass. Otherwise, it's surplus baggage.

About This Book

When this book was written as *Basic Essentials Map and Compass*, global positioning system (GPS) units were hot new items that only the well-heeled could afford. Now, prices have plummeted and a basic GPS model costs about the same as a high-end compass. The result is that people are buying GPS receivers like mad, though precious few people know how to use them. Many GPS owners view a compass as old fashioned and don't even carry one afield. They rely entirely on their GPS unit and think that's all they need.

The truth is, you must be proficient with a map and compass in order to take full advantage of GPS technology. Climb blindly onto the GPS bandwagon and you are certain to make mistakes when you use a GPS receiver.

For more than thirty years, I taught map and compass skills to eighth grade science students (this book evolved from that curriculum). I always introduced the unit with two questions:

"If I were to test you on twenty math problems and you got one wrong, what grade would you get?"

Answer: "Ninety-five and an A!"

"Now, imagine that you have to perform forty compass calculations while traveling through remote country. If you get one wrong, what do you get?

Answer: "Lost!"

The point is that you cannot afford to make a single mistake when you navigate. You *must* have a foolproof system for checking the data you transfer from your map to your compass or GPS unit and vice versa. Everyone makes mistakes, and you can't troubleshoot problems if you don't know the basics.

This book contains everything you need to know to travel confidently with map, compass, and GPS. This new edition includes a detailed section on GPS positioning and the popular UTM (Universal Transverse Mercator) coordinate reference system. You'll also find tips for choosing a compass and GPS unit and for avoiding common errors when using these instruments. Some GPS receivers now feature electronic digital compasses. Read why you shouldn't replace your needle compass with one!

May all your bearings be accurate and every course be true.

CHAPTER 1

Getting Started

Some years ago, while on a canoe trip in the Boundary Waters Canoe Area of Minnesota, I rounded a point and saw a young couple sitting dolefully on a rock, staring intently at what appeared to be a map. When they saw me, the pair stood up and waved frantically in my direction. Curiously, I paddled over, only to discover the two were hopelessly lost.

The man told me they'd left the lodge the day before and had set out with a complement of backpacking gear to hike a portion of the Kekakabic Trail—an old fire road that runs from Ely to Grand Marais. The trail crosses a number of area lakes, hence our chance meeting. But the trail is poorly marked, and it's not maintained. Numerous animal trails and canoe portages intersect the route and confuse things considerably. A good compass and topo map are essential tools for navigating the "Kek."

The man poured coffee while the woman continued to study the map. "I think we're here," she said, tapping her finger on what appeared to be a small knoll near the water's edge. Eagerly, she looked to me for reinforcement.

I squinted wonderingly at the impossibly small scale (1:500,000) map. Even with my bifocals, I could tell nothing.

"Where'd you get this map?" I questioned.

"From our outfitter," came the reply.

"Hmmm . . ." I walked back to the canoe and got my

1:24,000 topo map and spread it out on the lichen-splashed outcrop.

"I believe you're here," I said, pointing to a drumlin some distance from the perceived location. "How can you guys find your way around up here with a map like this?"

"We can't!" came the ready answer. "Our outfitter said this was all we needed, that it'd work fine."

"Yeah," I replied.

Fortunately, I had three sets of maps in my party, so parting with one caused no inconvenience.

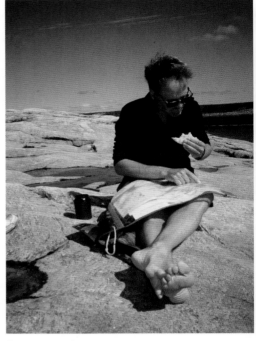

Reviewing the route.

As the case illustrates, you can't do good work without the right tools. A good map is everything. A compass alone won't do. A compass is useful only if you know where it leads you. And for that you need a map.

Even a simple state park or road map is better than no map at all. Example: Assume you're lost in a heavily wooded area. You have a compass but no map and no idea where you parked your car or "went in." Being lost comes as quite a surprise. After all, you hadn't planned on going in "that far."

Realistic problems? You bet! Ask any excited deer hunter. Think hard. How can you find your way out of the woods?

There is one way. It's called luck. Maybe if you go in a straight line (on any compass bearing) far enough, you'll hit a road. Maybe!

Now let's redo the problem with the aid of a highway map (figure 1-1). Only this time we can be more specific. You're cruising south on U.S. Highway 24 toward Leadville. You park somewhere along the roadway then strike off roughly northeast into the bush. You stuff map and compass deep into your pockets. Surely you won't need them. After all, you're going only "a short distance."

Several hours later, your enthusiasm dampens. Edged against a stand of impenetrable pines, miles of "nothing" stand between you and your car. Now what?

Your highway map shows that roads border the woods all around. Granted, there's not much detail, but it's enough. A rough southwest bearing will bring you back to US 24. From then on, it's simply a matter of asking directions.

As you can see, even a gas station highway map or state park guide will get you "out of the woods," if you have a compass and can use it for finding rough directions.

Beyond Planimetric Maps

The trouble with road maps (figure 1-1) and state park guides is that they're planimetric, which means they show topography in a dead-flat perspective. Hills and valleys don't mean much when you're driving a car. But put on your hiking boots and the mood suddenly changes. For cross-country—indeed any—wilderness travel, you need a map that shows all the ups and downs plus major stoppers such as swamps and

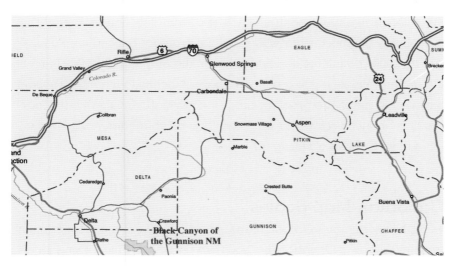

FIGURE 1-1:

Road map of the Glenwood Springs area.

canyon walls. Topographic maps, as they are called, provide a three-dimensional perspective of the land.

Topographic Maps

All modern maps are made from aerial photographs that give a precise picture of the land. Cartographers (mapmakers) use these photos to construct topographic maps in a variety of scales, the most common of which are summarized as follows.

American Map Scales

1:250,000 (1/250,000): One unit on the map equals 250,000 units on the ground. Each map covers one degree of latitude and two degrees of longitude (see discussion of latitude and longitude in the next section.) We Americans still work and think in the English system and our maps reflect our bias toward inches and feet. Here, 1 inch on the map equals 250,000 inches, or almost exactly 4 miles on the ground. As you might guess, one to a quarter-million maps don't show much detail.

1:62,500: Also called "15 minutes series," each map covers 15 minutes of latitude and 15 minutes of longitude. There are 63,360 inches to the mile, close enough so that 1 inch approximately equals 1 mile. This is probably the most useful and practical scale for backcountry use.

1:24,000 (7.5 minute series): 1 inch on the map equals 2,000 feet on the ground. Works out to a bit more than 2½ inches to the mile. These large-scale maps are great for precision navigation, but each one covers only about 55 square miles of territory, which means you'll need a lot of them if you're traveling far.

Canadian Map Scales

1:250,000 (same as American maps) and 1:50,000 are the most popular traveling maps in Canada. The 1:50s are particularly nice: Here, 1¼ inches equal one mile.

Special Map Features

Some American and Canadian maps offer additional useful features.

Colored or monochrome?

Canadian maps in 1:50,000 scale are often available in monochrome (black and white) as well as colored editions. Consequently, forests (commonly shown as green areas) and lakes (colored blue) will appear in varying shades of gray.

Why get monochrome maps if colored ones are available? Two reasons: they cost less and photocopy better—important considerations if you need a lot of maps or duplications of certain sheets.

Unfortunately, American maps are not available in monochrome editions.

Land Use Information Series maps

These are standard 1:250,000 Canadian topo maps that are over-printed with information about wildlife, vegetation, hunting and fishing, climate, and points of interest. They'll tell you where peregrine falcons nest, the migration routes and movements of caribou, the location of various fish species, and more. Land use maps tend to be cluttered with data, so they're only marginally useful for navigation.

These maps are not available for all of Canada. Ask for the special index to Land Use Information Series maps when you contact the Canada Map Office.

Land use and land cover maps

These American maps are similar to Canadian Land Use Information maps, with these exceptions: Land use refers to how man's activities affect the land (for example, housing and industry). Land cover describes the vegetation, water, and artificial constructions on the land surface. Scale is 1:100,000 or 1:250,000.

Where to Order Maps

You can't order maps until you know what's in print. For this, you'll need an Index to Topographic Maps, available free from the agencies below. You can write, phone, or e-mail your request for an index. Most agency Web sites now have interactive map indexes that allow you to simply point and click to find the map you need. The old-fashioned paper index may soon be a thing of the past.

U.S. Maps

U.S. Geological Survey (USGS)
Box 25286, Federal Center
Denver, CO 80225
(888) ASK USGS
(303) 202-4693 (fax)
www.usgs.gov.
The USGS is your complete source of U.S. topographic maps, aerial photos, and map-related publications. The new Map Locator on the Web site makes it easy to find the maps you need. If you don't have a computer, call and request a free index to the topographic maps in the state of your interest. The USGS accepts checks, money orders, and popular credit cards. You can order by phone or off the secure Web site.

National Oceanic and Atmospheric Administration (NOAA)
Communications and Education Division
1305 East-West Highway
Silver Spring, MD 20910
(301) 713-3060
www.nos.noaa.gov
NOAA offers charts and tide tables of U.S. coasts, the Great Lakes, sections of major rivers, and contoured fishing maps. You can search for maps, charts, and publications on NOAA's Web site.

Earth Science Information Center (ESIC)
(800) ASK USGS
http://geography.usgs.gov/esic/esic_index.html
Information specialists in this division of the USGS will answer questions and help you find special purpose maps, aerial photos (including space photos), and anything else you need. Search the ESIC's Web site or simply call.

Using Your Map

With your topo map in hand, you're ready to plan your route into the backcountry. Let's begin by identifying the important map features.

Map name: You'll find the map name in the upper and lower margins of American maps and in the lower margin of Canadian maps. American maps also have names in parentheses that indicate adjacent quadrangles. For example, the map just southeast of ASPEN, COLO. (figure 1-2) is NEW YORK PEAK.

The Canadians use a slightly different system (figure 1-3). Here, the NAKINA name and location designation (42L) are included in a dia-

Custom Maps of the United States

National Geographic topo!
National Geographic Maps
P.O. Box 4337
Evergreen, CO 80437-3457
800-962-1643
http://maps.nationalgeographic.com/topo
Detailed CD map sets that cover most of the United States. Back roads are available for some states; portages and campsites for the Boundary Waters Canoe Area of Minnesota. You choose the map scale, orientation, and coordinate system. Order maps or print your own.

www.mytopo.com
Build your own custom topographic map or aerial photograph of any area in the United States. Choose the scale, orientation, and coordinate system (latitude/longitude or UTM). Each map is printed on tough, waterproof Tyvek paper and shipped direct to you.

www.mymapcard.com
Map Card membership in "mytopo.com" allows you to customize, print, and download unlimited topo maps and aerial photographs on your computer.

Canadian Maps and Aerial Photos

Canada Map Office
615 Booth Street
Ottawa, ON, Canada K1A OE9
(800) 465-6277 or (613) 952-7000
www.maps.nrcan.gc.ca
Call the Canada Map Office and request an index to the topographic maps in the area you plan to travel. Or simply use the slick interactive index map on the CMO Web site to find the map you need. Note that the Canada Map Office no longer sells maps; instead, it lists dealers who do. However, you do order aerial photographs direct from the Canada Map Office. The Web site explains all. You are welcome to call if you have questions or don't have a computer.

Department of Fisheries and Oceans
Hydrographic Chart Distribution Office
1675 Russell Road, P.O. Box 8080
Ottawa, ON, Canada K1G 3H6
(613) 998-4931
(613) 998-1217 (fax)
www.charts.gc.ca
Canada's Department of Fisheries and Oceans publishes Canadian marine charts and tide tables. Orders must be placed through a Canadian map dealer.

gram in the legend—a procedure that allows you to see the adjacent map sheets at a glance.

Scale: You'll find the representative fraction (1:24,000, etc.) and bar scale in the lower map margin.

Date: Most topo maps are very old; some were last field-checked in the 1950s. A lot has changed since then, especially the location of roads, dams, and other man-made features. The key words revised and field-checked will tell you when these maps were last updated.

Certainly, an old topo map is better than none at all. But it won't do if you're planning a remote hunting or fishing trip. If you need more current information than that supplied by your map, contact the gov-

FIGURE 1-2:

Corner of a 1:24,000 map showing map name and adjacent southeast quadrangle.

FIGURE 1-3:

Index showing Nakina location and adjoining sheets on Canadian National Topographic System map.

FIGURE 1-4:

Lines of latitude run parallel to the equator. Lines of longitude run north-south and intersect at the poles.

FIGURE 1-5:

Latitude/Longitude of Denver.

ernment agency (U.S. Forest Service, Department of Natural Resources, etc.) nearest your area of concern. These professionals require current maps for their daily work. If they can't tell you where to get the maps you need, they'll help you update yours.

Latitude and longitude: Your map is a bird's-eye view of a tiny portion of the Earth's surface. But where does it fit onto the big sphere? By using latitude and longitude we can reference any location to a precise spot on the globe.

Lines of latitude (or parallels) run parallel to the equator, which is zero degrees. The longitudinal (north–south) lines that intersect at the poles are called meridians, or lines of longitude (figure 1-4). Longitude is measured in degrees east or west of the zero degree prime meridian, which originates in Greenwich, England.

By splitting latitude and longitude degree readings into smaller units, called minutes and seconds, specific points on the Earth may be accurately located via a coordinate system. The rules are simple:

1° (degree) = 60' (minutes)

1' (minute) = 60" (seconds)

For example, Denver (see figure 1-5) is located at approximately longitude 105° west / latitude 39°45' north.

All this is needlessly academic, unless you plan to order specific large-scale maps and aerial photographs.

Aerial Photos

Suppose you're planning to canoe a remote river in Canada. Your topo map says you'll have to portage your gear around a major falls along the route. The map does not tell you where the portage begins, however. In fact, the contour lines (more on this later) suggest there's an impassable canyon wall on both sides of the river.

Want to know more? Then order the aerial photographs from which your map was made. Photos will bring into clear perspective the most obscure features; more so if you specify stereo pairs. All you need is an inexpensive stereoscope (available at most hobby shops) to view the land in glorious 3-D. Now you'll find a route around the falls . . . if one exists!

For those who don't understand the ways of latitude and longitude: Outline your area of interest on a topo map and mail, fax, or scan and e-mail it, along with your payment, to the USGS or Canada Map Office. Your map will be returned with your order. Order aerial photos from the Canada Map Office, not from a topographic map dealer.

Which Way Is North?

"North," as everyone who has headed "up" north knows, is always at the top of the map. Well, sort of. And for conventional route finding in

FIGURE 1-6:

Locating a true north-south meridian.

the American Midwest, you can get by with that knowledge alone. However, if you plan to travel in the East or West, you'll need to take into account the differences between the three norths.

Most important is true, or geographical, north. That's the direction in which the lines of longitude run. Since the vertical lines that describe the right and left map margins are true meridians, any line on your map drawn parallel to them runs true north and south. Almost!

Meridians converge toward the poles, so the ones that run along your map edges are not truly parallel to one another (and the closer you get to each pole, the less parallel they become). No problem; that's what the "neat lines" are for.

Neat lines appear as tiny tick marks at equidistant points along all four map margins. To locate a true north–south meridian, simply con-nect the neat lines of equal value at the top and bottom of the map (figure 1-6 shows the relationship). Similarly, you can plot a true east–west line (parallel) by connecting the latitude neat lines. Then you can use these coordinates to accurately plot the latitude and longitude of any point on your map.

The Other Norths

Grid north: All topographic maps have grid lines imprinted on their faces. Grid lines began life as true meridians and parallels but became distorted when the spherical Earth was portrayed flat on paper. Cartographers use a number of map projections to minimize this distortion, but all are subject to some small error. Consequently, grid lines usually do not point true north–south or true east–west. The error is reported in a declination diagram (refer to figure 4-8) in the bottom map margin, and the error is usually small enough that it can be ignored by everyone but surveyors.

Grid north is the north you'll want to use when working with civilian and military topographic maps. Use true north with maps that don't have grid lines imprinted on their faces.

Magnetic north: Most everyone knows that the compass needle does not point to true north. Rather, it points toward the north magnetic pole that is located several hundred miles south of the real thing.

The angular difference between the "three norths" is reported in declination diagrams or legend information on all topographic maps. In chapter 4 we'll have a lively discussion of how this affects navigation.

Contour Lines

The thin brown lines on topographic maps are called contour lines. They give "depth" and elevation to the land. You'll learn all about them in the next chapter.

> **Tip:**
> If you have an old map, don't take the location of trails, unimproved roads, churches, and schools too seriously. It's quite possible that some of these man-made features no longer exist!

Map Symbols

How do you tell (on a map) a school from a church? By the appropriate symbol, of course. There are dozens of map symbols, most of which are obvious. But lest you forget, Canadian maps emblazon them all in the margin or on the back. American USGS maps are more subtle. They tease you with a few road classifications, then assume you know the rest or have on hand their free pamphlet Topographic Map Symbols, which lists them all.

You'll find a listing of the most common symbols in appendix 1. The USGS Web site (specifically, http://erg.usgs.gov/isb/pubs/booklets/symbols) gives all the symbols.

You should also realize that, for clarity, map symbols are not drawn to scale—they always appear much larger than they really are. However, the *geometric center* of these symbols is accurately plotted. So shoot a compass bearing (or measure) there if you need to target a particular point.

CHAPTER 2

Easy Map Reading

Understanding Map Contours

The light brown lines overprinted on topographic maps are called *contour* lines. They indicate the elevation above sea level (sometimes other references are used) of land features and thus permit you to view the topography in three dimensions instead of two. Entire books have been written about contour lines and their interpretation; however, you'll get along quite nicely if you master these basics:

1. Contour lines connect points of *equal* elevation. Thus, closely spaced lines indicate lots of elevation change, whereas widely spaced lines show the opposite (figure

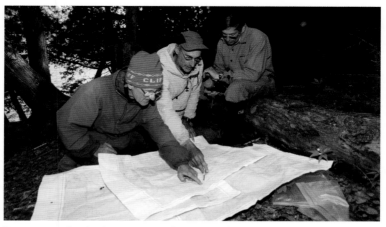

A canoeist checks his position. Along the Steel River in Ontario, Canada.

2-1). You gain or lose elevation only when you travel from one contour line to another. If you walk along a contour line, you'll be "on the level."

2. The *contour interval* (CI) is the vertical distance between contour lines. Its value in feet or meters is given in the lower map margin. Thus, if the CI is 50 feet, each successive contour line on the map increases or decreases (as the case may be) in elevation by exactly 50 feet. Each *fifth "index"* contour line is dark colored and is labeled with a number that gives its actual elevation above sea level.

3. The contour interval is determined by the cartographer, based on the amount of elevation change in the area. Mountainous regions will have a contour interval of 50 feet or more, while on relative flatlands it may be 10 feet or less. Consequently, the contour interval *is not the same* for all maps.

FIGURE 2-1

Contour lines: Mountain Island. CI=25 ft.

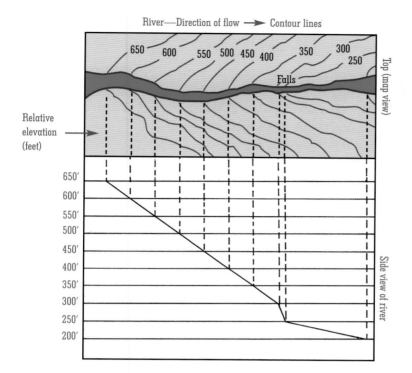

River—Direction of flow ➤ Contour lines

650 600 550 500 450 400 350 300 250

Falls

Top (map view)

Relative elevation (feet)

650'
600'
550'
500'
450'
400'
350'
300'
250'
200'

Side view of river

FIGURE 2-2

Falls are easy to spot on the contour map. Closely spaced vee points indicate a sudden drop. Notice the difference between the extreme elevation change at 300' to 250' and the long decline between 250' and 200'.

4.   The larger the contour interval, the less clear are the characteristics of the area. In short, a map with a CI of 10 feet gives a clearer picture of the topography than one with a CI of 100 feet. Keep this fact uppermost in your mind when you plan a cross-country hiking or ski trip. Remember, the shortest distance between two points is a straight line only if you're not mountain climbing!

5.   Where contour lines cross or run very close together, you'll find an abrupt drop—a falls or canyon (figure 2-2). Especially look for these closely spaced contour lines if you're boating an unknown river. If tight contours *intersect* your route, you can bet there are substantial rapids there.

To allay your concern, you may want to plot a river *profile* that shows the actual drop per mile.

6. The closed or vee end of a contour line always points upstream (figures 2-2, 2-4). Note that this rule also applies to creeks, intermittent streams, and gullies.
7. Contour lines become U-shaped (the closed ends of the U's point *downhill*) to indicate the outjutting spur (ridge) of a hill.
8. The actual heights of many objects are given on topographic maps. For example, suppose you find the number 636X printed at a road junction. This means that the X-marked spot is exactly 636 feet (or meters, as the case may be) above sea level.

Making the Map Profile

Begin by drawing a broad line along each side of the river, parallel to your route. These lines reference your route—and draw your eyes to the river—so you can quickly locate what lies ahead, without visual interference from other map features. I use a translucent felt-tip highlighter pen.

Next, consult the map scale and mark the miles along your route. Gear the number of markers to the map scale. For example, on 1:250,000 maps, I label every 4 miles (figure 2-3), which works out to a mark every inch. On larger-scale maps I tick off each mile. The idea is to clarify without cluttering.

Now get your pencil and draw a small arrow everywhere a contour line crosses the river. Write in the elevations of each contour near the penciled arrow and circle it. Be sure you indicate whether the elevation is in feet or meters.

You're now ready to compute the *drop*. Do the computations in a table similar to that in figure 2-3. For example, the 800-foot contour crosses the river at mile 63, while the 700-foot line intersects at mile 69.

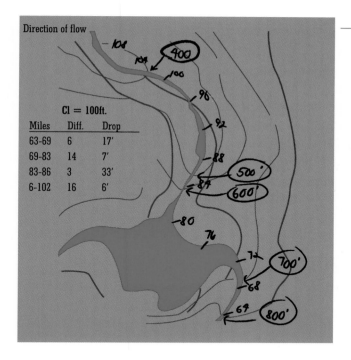

Direction of flow

CI = 100ft.

Miles	Diff.	Drop
63-69	6	17'
69-83	14	7'
83-86	3	33'
6-102	16	6'

FIGURE 2-3

The map profile illustrates the techniques used to determine the drop of a typical river. Handwritten circled numbers indicate contours. Distances (miles) are not circled.

This is recorded in the table as 63-69. The mileage difference is six (69-63). Dividing six into 100 (the value of the contour interval) yields a drop of 17 feet per mile.

From mile 69 to 83 the river drops less—7 feet per mile, etc.

In deciding if it's safe to boat an unknown river, keep these rules of thumb in mind:

1. A drop of 3 to 5 feet per mile is nice cruising for an open canoe or fishing boat. Ten feet per mile means gentle rapids. Twenty or more is about the limit of an open canoe, and 35 may mean you'll have to portage your rubber raft. Caution: These are only guidelines. Maps tell you what to expect—not *what is!* Use your eyes to account for that.

2. Equally important as drop per mile is how the drops occur— whether uniformly or at a falls, dam, or major rapid. Closely spaced drops mean a probable portage at those spots, though the rest of the river may be "user friendly." Uniform drops suggest a wild, fast ride, and your skills had best be up to it!

Note:

You can convert the "top view" of your profile to a side view for greater clarity. Figure 2-2 shows the procedure. You can also use this same method to draw a profile for land masses. Suppose you want to hike cross-country, but a large hill stands in the way. Can you walk the hill, or will you have to crawl up it? To find out the answer, simply draw a line from your location to your destination, and graph the drop as shown in figure 2-2. Or scan the map section into your computer and let a mapping softwear program do the work. Another method: Assign a GPS waypoint (more on this later) to each place that a contour line crosses the river. Then use an online mapping program, such as GPS Visualizer (www.gpsvisualizer.com/profile) to graph the drop.

Contour Quiz

Use figure 2-5 to test your knowledge of contour lines. Answers are at the end of the quiz.

1. Is the creek flowing *into* or *out* of Pikitigushi Lake?
2. You are standing at point A. What is your height above sea level? (Clue: Notice the 1,000-foot contour to the east.)
3. You are standing at point B, looking toward Pikitigushi Lake. Describe the topography directly in front of you.
4. You are walking south, from B to C. Are you: gaining elevation? losing elevation? remaining level?
5. You walk from B to D. Are you: going up a steep hill? going down a gully? going up a gully?
6. A creek joins lake E from the west. Does that creek flow *into* or *out* of lake E?

Answers to Contour Quiz

1. Into the lake. Remember, the closed ends of a contour line point *upstream*.
2. 1,250 feet. The index contour to the east is labeled 1,000. The contour interval is 50 feet; 50 feet x 5 lines = 250 feet of rise.
3. Very steep drop, almost a cliff. You wouldn't want to climb it.
4. You lose 50 feet of elevation (you go down 100 feet to the plateau, then climb 50 feet to reach C).

5. Down a gully.

6. The creek flows *to the west*, out of lake E.

Using the Bar Scale to Measure Horizontal Distances

Most of the time, maintaining map–ground scale relationships is simply a matter of remembering how many inches per mile the scale portrays and interpolating accordingly. However, sometimes you want a more precise answer than your guesstimate provides. One way is to use the bar scale in the map legend and a piece of scratch paper.

To compute the distance from A to B in figure 2-6, place the paper edge between the points and transfer this distance to the scale below. You'll get a bit more then ⁹⁄₁₀ of a mile.

You can also measure the distance directly with the graduated baseplate of your orienteering compass.

FIGURE 2-4

1. Creek A flows into river at point B.

2. River flows from B to C.

River

Direction of flow

Creek **A** flows into river **B** below

Closed end of contour line always points upstream

Direction of flow

FIGURE 2-5

Contour quiz illustration.

CONTOUR INTERVAL 50 FEET
Elevations in feet above mean sea level
North American datum 1927
Transverse mercator projection

Preparing Your Maps for Use in the Backcountry

Maps are a joy to use if they're well organized and protected from the weather. Here are the recommended procedures:

1. Begin by outlining your route with a felt-tip highlighter. This way you can see where you're going at a glance.

2. If you're hiking or boating on a river or lake, you'll want to tick off the miles, as explained on pages 18–20, "Making the Map Profile." This will keep you from biting off more than you can swallow when you do your winter planning. Canoeists, kayakers, and rafters should carefully designate the location of stoppers such as falls and dangerous rapids and the positioning of portage trails. To allay your concern, you may want to draw a river (or trail) profile that shows the actual drop per mile.

3. Maps that will be frequently used in fishing boats are best glued to a thin plywood board, then clear lacquered to protect them from water. Drill a hole in one corner of the board and attach a nylon security cord. You may also want to tie your compass to the board. Now everything is at hand and protected from the elements.

Here are other ways to waterproof your maps:

1. Insert them in zipper-lock plastic bags. Giant 12-½-by-16-inch zipper-lock bags are available from office supply stores. Camping equipment shops (and most Boy Scout supply centers) carry heavier, similar-sized plastic envelopes with genuine zippers. If you want an inexpensive giant-sized map case, check out your local bait shop. Four-mil-thick "minnow" bags measure 32-by-17-½-inches (these are also great for sleeping bags and clothing). Seal the mouth of each bag with duct tape.

2. Aloksak waterproof plastic bags make great map cases. These inexpensive plastic bags look like ordinary zipper-lock bags, but they are much stronger and are waterproof to depths exceeding 196 feet, even when placed under mild compression. They have a patented triple seal and come in sizes to fit everything from pass-

FIGURE 2-6

Mark the location of A and B on your paper, then compare it to the map bar scale.

ports and cell phones to topographic maps and bulky clothes. (See appendix 4.)

3. A commercial map case is worth having. Cooke Custom Sewing, Forestry Suppliers, and Watchfuleye Designs have excellent ones. (See appendix 4)

4. Cover maps with clear contact paper—it makes them waterproof, but you can't write on them.

5. Paint on Stormproof—a clear chemical that's formulated for use on maps and charts. Most camping shops have it. Or apply Thompson's Water Seal—an industrial-strength chemical that's used for sealing concrete blocks. TWS is available in hardware stores in aerosol cans and tins. Apply it with a foam varnish brush. TWS (and Stormproof) makes maps water repellent, not water-proof. You can write over it with pen or pencil.

6. No sense carrying map portions that you won't use. So trim away unnecessary paper with a scissors before you leave home. *Important*: Don't remove important margin data that you may need for navigation! If you travel by compass, you'll want, at the very least, the magnetic declination diagram and contour interval. GPS users will need the map datum and zone, the latitude/longitude, and UTM coordinate values. Chapter 6 explains all.

7. If you have a number of map sheets, use either of these methods for organizing them:

• Glue the quadrangles together with rubber cement, accurately matching the latitude/longitude neat lines. Cut out important legend information and glue it to the map back or over a nonessential area.

• Number individual map sheets consecutively. This works fine, except when you find yourself at the edge of a map sheet.

Maps that will be used in the field are better folded than rolled.

Tip:
Forestry Suppliers, in Jackson, Mississippi (see appendix 4), carries a complete line of tools for the professional forester and geologist, including map aids and laminating films for maps and journals. It carries the complete line of Silva, Suunto, Nexus, and Brunton compasses.

CHAPTER 3

Anatomy of the Compass

No one is certain where or how the compass originated, though it appears that the Chinese were first to discover magnetism in lodestone and its attractive power. One of the first working models consisted of a piece of lodestone floating on a cork in a bowl of water. Other primitive compasses, with magnets shaped like fish or turtles, can be seen in Chinese books that date from the eleventh and twelfth centuries.

The first clear description of a magnetic-needle compass is by Shen Kua, a Chinese, in a.d. 1088—about a century before the earliest mention in European texts. From then on, there are numerous references to compasses in Chinese literature as well as stories about their use by sailors "in dark weather or when the sky is overcast." Other references suggest that primitive compasses were used by Arabian merchants in a.d. 1200 and by Vikings a half century later.

It is not clear whether magnetism and its use for navigation was discovered independently in Europe or brought by travelers from China.

For a while the Chinese led the world in compass production, evidently because the hardened steel needed to hold the magnetism was not available in other parts of the world. But around 1400–1500, Europeans got into the act, and marine compasses became widely available. However, it wasn't until someone realized that compasses could be modified into sundials—and thereby substitute for the expensive watches of the day—that portable field compasses were born.

Little change took place until the end of the pocket sundial period, around 1750. Then came the development of sighting devices and the refinement of the "watch" or "box" compass, which survives today with few modifications.

The twentieth century saw substantial improvements in field compasses in the form of the Bezard compass of 1902 and the liquid-filled British Army compass of World War I. But it was not until the 1930s that the real excitement began. First came the development of reasonably priced, liquid-filled orienteering compasses and birth of the Silva company, then the introduction of protractor-combined plate compasses and sophisticated sighting devices. Things continue on the upswing in the twenty-first century: The best of today's compasses are a tribute to engineering genius—a quiet lesson in sophisticated simplicity. (I am indebted to Björn Kjellstrom, inventor of the Silva compass, for this historical information.)

Modern Compasses

A century ago route finding was a precarious business. Maps of wilderness areas were not always accurate, and compasses were heavy, slow to use, not waterproof, and had no provision for computing bearings from a map.

Now all that has changed. The best modern compasses incorporate complete navigational systems. No longer do you have to grope for a pencil and protractor and orient the map to north to take a bearing. And don't let the plastic toylike construction of these instruments fool you. Most of the mid-priced ($15–$25) models can be consistently read to within 2 degrees of an optical transit—hand held! Even the cheapies seldom vary by more than 4 degrees.

There are five types of modern compasses: 1) *fixed dial* or *standard needle*, 2) *floating dial*, 3) *cruiser*, 4) *orienteering*, and 5) *electronic*. There's also the braille compass—actually developed from the floating-dial format. For hiking, canoeing, hunting, fishing, and just about everything else, only the orienteering type (and where extreme accuracy is required, the floating dial with optical sights) makes much sense. Here are the differences:

Fixed-Dial Compass

Best typified by twenty-five-cent gumball machine models, these questionably superior versions of the old box compass have degree readings embossed on a fixed

FIGURE 3-1

Fixed-dial compass.

outer ring (figure 3-1). The needle rides on a hardened steel or mineral bearing in the center of the capsule. Fixed-dial compasses are slow to use, inaccurate, and not very versatile. People buy them because they don't know how to use any other kind. About all these are good for is zipper pulls on jackets. Nonetheless, because they are so popular, you should know how to use them effectively. You'll find the specifics on page 37.

Floating-Dial Compass

The needle is an integral part of the numbered dial and spins freely on the pivot. You point the compass toward your objective and read the bearing at an index. There's nothing to set, usually, not even a cover to raise. Floating-dial compasses run the gauntlet of quality—from the five-dollar "hunter pin-on" to

FIGURE 3-2

Suunto KB-14, an optical sighting, Floating-dial sighting compass.

sophisticated direct sighting models like the Suunto KB-14 (figure 3-2) that can be interpolated to more than 15 minutes of arc.

Marine compasses (figure 3-3)—like those used on small powerboats and kayaks—are usually of the floating-dial type. Their advantage is that they provide an instant bearing. You don't need to take your hands off the tiller or paddle to use them.

FIGURE 3-3

A simple floating-dial compass mounted on a canoe thwart.

Cruiser Compasses

These are professional-grade instruments (figure 3-4) that come in solid metal cases with protective hinged covers, onto which a "lubber's" (sighting) line has been inscribed. Numbers on the dial run counterclockwise (opposite to that of a fixed-dial compass) so you

FIGURE 3-4

Sighting a Brunton Pocket Transit, a cruiser-style compass.

can face your objective and the instrument where the north end of the magnetic needle intersects the dial.

Despite their dated design, "cruisers" are still used by foresters and geologists. They are accurate, heavy, slow to use, not waterproof, and very expensive.

FIGURE 3-5

A Silva Ranger orienteering compass with hinged sighting mirror. (Photo: Silva Company)

Orienteering Compasses—The Choice of Serious Outdoorspeople

Accuracy is only half the game. The other part is determining what numerical value to set on the compass. For this, you need a map and protractor.

Enter the *orienteering* compass (figure 3-5). In 1933 Gunnar Tillander, an unemployed instrument worker, approached Björn Kjellstrom and his brothers Alvar and Arvid with a unique plan: Why not incorporate a pro-tractor into the design of a standard needle compass? Almost overnight, the orienteering compass was born. It is unique for these reasons:

1. You can determine bearings from a map *without* the aid of a protractor and without orienting the map to north. This means you can make the computation from the seat of a bob-bing canoe or while shuffling down a wilderness trail. You can even do it with mittens on!

FIGURE 3-6

Silva Cobalt digital compass. Note the built-in baseplate for transfer-ring bearings from map to com-pass. (Photo: Silva Company)

2. Your direction of travel (bearing) is "locked" onto the compass dial. There's nothing to remember or write down. In fact, you don't even have to read the dial at all!

3. All orienteering compasses have ruled scales along their plastic baseplates that make it easy to determine scale distances from a map.

4. Orienteering compasses all have liquid-damped needles. Needle oscillation ceases in three to five seconds. The system works in temperatures down to 40 below zero.

5. The instrument is so simple that an eight-year-old can learn to run one in a matter of minutes.

For backcountry use, the orienteering compass has no peer. Unless you're running survey lines in search of buried treasure—in which case, you'll want an optical sighting compass—I can think of no reason why you should choose any other kind.

Because the orienteering compass is so versatile, the instruction in this book is centered around its use.

Electronic Digital Compasses

Technology has brought about a number of electronic compasses (figure 3-6). Some have a memory and chronograph, plus an automatic shut-off switch to prevent battery drain. A few digital watches feature miniature electronic compasses, but none are accurate or versatile enough for serious navigation.

The best digital compasses are as accurate as the best needle compasses, and their bearings are much easier to read. The bad part is that electronic compasses are powered by batteries, which can fail, and electronic models don't have built-in protractors to obtain map bearings and distances. This rules them out for backcountry use.

Unlike a needle compass, an electronic compass must be recalibrated every time you change batteries or move very far from its previously calibrated location. To recalibrate, you rotate the instrument (usually twice) 360 degrees—full circle. The compass must be held dead level during rotation. Sound bizarre? It is! If you go out of calibration range and forget to recalibrate, you're lost! Running by e-compass also consumes some battery power. Needle compasses point for free.

At this writing, only one electronic model—the Silva Cobalt digital compass—has an orienteering style baseplate that allows bearings to be computed from a map.

Braille Compass

Silva of Sweden makes the world's only braille compass, which the Brunton company distributes under the Nexus name (figure 3-7). It uses a floating-compass card (floating-dial model) with braille markings. When the cover is closed, the compass card turns freely; when opened, the dial and bearing are locked in place.

FIGURE 3-7

A Brunton Nexus model 16B compass. When the cover is closed, the compass card turns freely; when opened, the dial and bearing lock in place. (Photo: Silva Company)

Accuracy: How Much Do You Need?

Surveyors and foresters need compasses that give readings to a fraction of a degree. But for general outdoor use, any instrument that will consistently read within 4 degrees of a transit will do, even for serious expeditions. You don't need 30-minute accuracy for navigating the backcountry. What you do need is a good map and versatile compass.

Consider this: One degree of compass error equals 92 feet per mile (tangent 1° x 5,280) of ground error. A 4-degree error over a mile course will cause you to miss your objective by 368 feet—hardly significant when you consider how compasses are actually used. For example, rather than risk missing their objective (even by 368 feet), experienced travelers "aim off." That is, they make a purposeful error to the left or right of the reference point. Then they follow a road, trail, shoreline, power line, or other "handrail" to their destination. Figure 4-7 in the next chapter details the procedure.

Aiming off becomes even more important when you realize that manmade features such as buildings and trails are frequently misplotted on maps. Under these conditions, clear thinking is more important than precise headings. Here's what you need most in a working compass:

1. **Versatility** in transferring bearings from map to ground—hence, the desirability of the orienteering compass.

2. **Speed of operation:** Often, you need to determine a direction from the seat of a bobbing canoe or kayak.

3. **Carryability:** Consider your compass to be an article of clothing, one you'll wear all the time. The lighter and more compact the instrument, the more pleasurable it will be to carry. Particularly shun the compass with sharp, square edges. Square corners may be great for map plotting, but they'll eat through your clothes in a matter of minutes.

4. **Durability:** I once had a jeep run over an old Silva Ranger. The cover was smashed, but the instrument worked fine. That's tough! A field compass must be built to take everything from a bad fall to a thorough dousing.

5. **Amenities:** Are the scales on the baseplate compatible with those on your map? Can the compass be compensated for area magnetic declination? (See chapter 4 for details.) Night sights—either luminous or (better) a tritium light—are essential for black night travel. And if you're over age forty, a built-in magnifying glass will clarify map subtleties.

Damping

A compass needle will continue to oscillate for some time unless it is damped, either by a light-viscosity liquid (*liquid damping*) or by magnetism (*induction damping*). Liquid-damped needles will stop moving in about three seconds; induction-damped needles take much longer. As to longevity, the vote goes to induction damping, as there's never a chance for a leaky capsule.

Figure 3-8

Characteristics of compass styles.

Compass Type	Probable Maximum Error without Practice	Probable Maximum Error with Considerable Practice	Approximate Time to Take an Accurate Bearing
Optical sighting	1 degree	½ degree or less	15 seconds
Orienteering	4 degrees	1½ degrees	10 seconds
Induction-damped cruiser	4 degrees	1½ degrees	20 seconds
Liquid-damped fixed dial	10 degrees	5 degrees	15 seconds

However, induction-damped instruments are usually heavier, bulkier, and more expensive than liquid-damped ones. Nearly all the best hand compasses are currently liquid filled. Except for the Brunton Pocket Transit professional model, induction damping has all but disappeared from the compass scene.

Sights

Some compasses come equipped with sights, which may or may not be a good thing.

Optical (lensatic and prismatic) sights are most accurate and, in compasses of good quality, give results comparable to expensive surveying instruments. When you look through an optical sight, you see image, graduated dial, and a vertical intersect line, all in the same plane. The result, in a well-built compass, is accuracy to a fraction of a degree.

Lensatic sights, like those on the old military field compass, are good or bad, depending on the precision of the sight assembly. The original U.S. Army lensatics could be read to 2 degrees of perfection or better. But the ten-dollar foreign copies that currently flood the market are another matter. Most won't read within 5 degrees of a transit!

Combination mirror-vee sights have a pop-up mirror with a vertical line scribed through its center. You adjust the mirror to a 60-degree angle (so you can see the alignment of the needle in the capsule), turn your body (not the compass) until the needle is centered within a printed arrow on the dial, then peer across the gunsight vee on the cover top toward your objective. Sounds accurate, and it can be, if you're extremely meticulous. Fact is, you can do as well—often better— by simply holding the instrument waist high and looking straight ahead. Accuracy of the system depends in large measure on precision mounting of the mirror and your ability to keep everything in alignment while holding it all rock steady.

The problem with *all* nonoptical sights is their very short sighting plane—akin to shooting accurately a pistol with a 2-inch barrel. As explained, the accuracy of any sight depends on the precision and ruggedness of the mounting system. Unfortunately, most hinged compass sights lack the durability for long-term precise alignment. For this reason, your best bet is to use the waist-high method of sighting that is explained at the end of this chapter. Still, a hinged cover is nice because it protects the compass lens from knocks and scratches.

Declination

Some compasses have a mechanical adjustment for magnetic declination. This feature is quite inexpensive and is necessary only if you live in an area where declination values are large, or if you are confused by the mathematics of its computation. See the next chapter for details.

Inclination

The Earth behaves like a giant magnet, and the closer you get to the poles, the greater the magnetic force. This causes the north end of the needle to tip down in the Northern Hemisphere and to rise in the Southern Hemisphere. Consequently, the compass needle must be balanced for the zone of operation so the needle will spin freely on its pivot.

Professional surveying instruments have a movable counterweight on the needle tail that can be repositioned if necessary. Field compasses, however, come from the factory balanced for the zone of use. Most any compass you buy in the United States will work fine in North

America. Hiking in Ecuador is another matter! Instruments that are balanced for far northern and southern zones are available on special order from the best compass makers.

Dial Graduations

The best compasses have dials that are graduated in 1- or 2-degree increments. Having more graduations than this simply clutters the dial. However, a lot of fine instruments have 5-degree graduations (especially those with small dials), and this is quite suitable for a field compass.

The rule is that you can interpolate a bearing by twice splitting the distance between the graduations on either side of the index. Thus, a 2-degree dial can be guesstimated to ½ degree; a 5-degree dial to 1¼ degrees, etc. So if you need the most precise readings, opt for finer graduations.

It's important to realize that precision bearings are only useful when combined with optical sighting systems. They are of little value in an orienteering compass. That's because orienteering instruments are almost never "read." Instead, the needle is aligned in the "doghouse" (printed arrow inside the capsule) and the direction-of-travel arrow on the baseplate is followed. There is no need to read specific numbers. Indeed, orienteering compasses need not be graduated at all.

How Much Does a Good Compass Cost?

At this writing, twenty bucks will buy all the compass you need for wilderness travel. Paying more won't necessarily buy more accuracy or versatility. Options such as declination adjustments, night sights, and sighting devices drive up costs and add little utility. Fact is, the least expensive orienteering models are suitable for the most complex lake and land navigation you're likely to encounter. You don't need a professional compass for touring the backcountry.

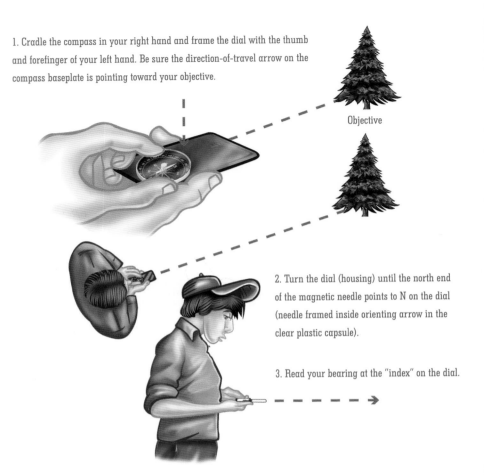

1. Cradle the compass in your right hand and frame the dial with the thumb and forefinger of your left hand. Be sure the direction-of-travel arrow on the compass baseplate is pointing toward your objective.

Objective

2. Turn the dial (housing) until the north end of the magnetic needle points to N on the dial (needle framed inside orienting arrow in the clear plastic capsule).

3. Read your bearing at the "index" on the dial.

FIGURE 3-9

Read compass at index described on dial.

How to Use the Waist-High Method of Sighting Your Orienteering Compass

Here's the most accurate way to take a bearing to a distant object with an orienteering compass:

Cradle the compass in your right hand and frame the dial with the thumb and forefinger of your left hand (figure 3-9). Forearms should be held gently but firmly against the body to provide a three-point (triangular) position, the apex of which is the compass.

Locate the compass *directly* along the midline of your body, just above your waist and a comfortable distance (about 6 inches) away from your stomach.

Next, turn your body (*not the compass*) until the direction-of-travel arrow on the compass baseplate is pointing toward the objective whose bearing you want to determine. Then, while holding the baseplate steady, turn the compass housing until the magnetic needle is framed inside the orienting arrow doghouse in the clear plastic capsule.

Now, take three "eye-shift" readings to your objective; that is, sight three times from the compass housing to the objective, *without* moving your head. When the alignment of everything—needle in doghouse, direction-of-travel arrow, and objective—is perfect, read your bearing. It should be within 2 degrees of an optical transit.

How to Take an Accurate Bearing with a Fixed-Dial Compass

Although experienced wilderness travelers rely entirely on orienteering-style compasses, they frequently carry a small gumball machine

Read your bearing here.

FIGURE 3-10

A fixed-dial compass can be used to take a reasonably accurate bearing if you use this procedure.

compass as an emergency backup. Even a simple zipper-pull compass can provide accurate directions if you know how to use it. Here's the recommended procedure:

1. Squarely face the objective whose bearing you wish to determine, then frame the compass between your thumbs and forefingers, as illustrated in figure 3-10. Your index fingers form a triangle, the apex of which points to the objective.

2. Rotate the compass between your fingers until the north end of the magnetic needle points to north on the dial.

3. Hold everything rock steady and read your bearing at the point where your forefingers touch. You should be within 5 degrees of a transit.

Now that you've mastered the workings of map and compass, you're ready to use them together as a complete navigational system. The next chapter shows you how.

CHAPTER 4

Navigation Basics

First, Some Compass Basics

The compass is graduated in degrees. There are 360 degrees in the compass circle, or rose (figure 4-1). The cardinal directions (north, south, east, and west) are each 90 degrees apart. Memorize the eight principal points of the compass and their relationship to the map. This will help eliminate the most common of compass errors—the 180-degree error.

For example: Assume you are fishing Lost Lake (figure 4-2) and are anchored at the peninsula at point E. You want to go to Mud Island, which lies 1½ miles to the east. With your orienteering compass you inadvertently compute a bearing of 270

FIGURE 4-1

The compass rose.

FIGURE 4-2

Lost Lake practice map.

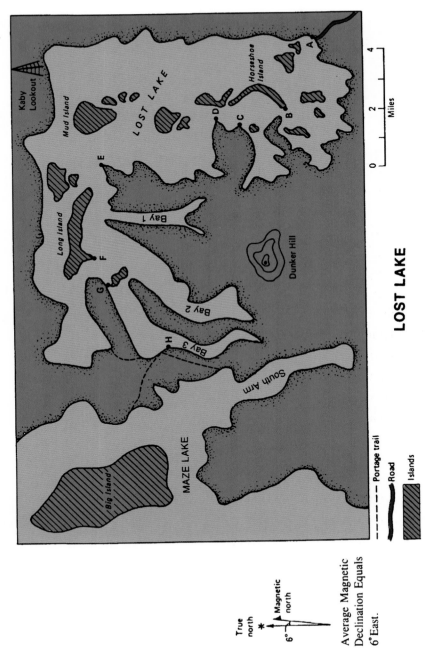

LOST LAKE

degrees, which is 180 degrees in error. However, if you had mentally superimposed the compass rose over point E before you determined the map bearing to the island, you'd have instantly discovered your mistake.

It is not uncommon to transfer data from map to compass and make serious directional mistakes. *A knowledge of your approximate direction of travel should be known before you get down to specifics!*

Using the Compass to Determine a Map Bearing

A bearing is one of the 360-degree directions of the compass rose. It is always measured *clockwise* from north (either true, grid, or magnetic) to the place you want to go (your objective). For now, we'll forget about the differences between the "three norths" and simply reference our bearing to true north, that is, at the top of the Lost Lake map in figure 4-2.

Assume you plan to fish the south end of Long Island on Lost Lake. Getting to Long Island from your location at A should be easy: Just head north up the east shoreline, counting bays as you go. When you see Mud Island, hang a left around the north edge and you'll run right into your treasure spot. Easy as pie.

Don't you believe it! Look at the map scale. It's more than 12 miles to Long Island. Even on a clear day, it's doubtful you'll be able to see the intermediate islands or bays along the way. Islands and shoreline will blend to oneness. Because of wind and waves you'll lose all sense of distance traveled. You can easily mistake one of the closer islands for Mud Island, or you can get turned around completely and become convinced that a channel between islands is a large bay, or vice versa.

But getting to Long Island is easy if you have a systematic plan and a compass. The important thing is to keep track of where you are all the time—easy enough if you compute bearings to intermediate checkpoints along the way and reaffirm your position at each point. Here's the procedure:

First, pick a checkpoint on the map. It should be some place that's reasonably close and easily identifiable—a small island, the tip of a peninsula, a prominent bay, etc. You may or may not be able to see these checkpoints (or *attack points*, as they're called in orienteering terms) from your location at A.

You decide that your first attack point will be the southern tip of Horseshoe Island, 2¾ miles away. Begin by guesstimating the bearing from your location at A to your objective at B. You'll be heading northwest, or about 315 degrees. Remember that number!

Next, determine the actual compass bearing from A to B, with your orienteering compass (preferred) or a protractor.

Protractor Method

Use this if you don't have an orienteering compass.

1. Draw a line from A to B.
2. Center your protractor over A and align "protractor north" with true north on your map (figure 4-3). Remember, true north is at the top of your map. Its direction is indicated by the starred leg of the declination diagram (more on this later) in the right map margin.
3. Read the protractor at the line intersect. You get 290 degrees.
4. Compare this figure (290 degrees) with your guesstimate of 315 degrees. Are the two within 90 degrees of one another? Good. You haven't made an error: You know you're going in the right direction!

Orienteering-Compass Method

1. Place either the left or right edge of the compass baseplate over point A. Place the forward edge of the same side of the baseplate on point B. Your compass is now pointing in the direction you want to go—from A to B, not from B to A (figure 4-4).
2. *While holding the baseplate tightly in position*, turn the compass housing until north on the dial points to the top (true north) of the map. Caution: Don't use the magnetic needle! Your direction of travel—290 degrees—is now locked onto the dial and can be read at the index inscribed on the compass base.
3. Now . . . while holding the compass in front of you with the direction-of-travel arrow inscribed on the base pointing away from your body, rotate your body with the compass until the magnetic

FIGURE 4-3

*Using a protractor
to determine a
map bearing.*

LOST LAKE

Horseshoe
Island

YOU MUST DRAW
A LINE FROM
A TO B.

B

Bearing of line A-B
equals 290°

needle points to north on the dial. Look straight ahead. You are
now facing 290 degrees—toward Horseshoe Island.

4. All that's necessary now is to locate a notch or visible incongruity
on the horizon that you can identify as being on this course of
travel. Put your compass away, fire up your motor, and cruise
toward your objective.

Okay, test time. Use your orienteering compass or protractor to compute the true bearings from points A through H on the Lost Lake map.
Check your answers in figure 4-5. Don't try to compute distance, travel
time, or magnetic bearing. We'll get to these later.

Azimuth and Bearing

The terms *azimuth* and *bearing* are often used interchangeably to indicate one of the 360-degree directions of the compass rose. *Bearing* is
the most common term so I have used it exclusively in this book, even

FIGURE 4-4

How to align an orienteering compass on a map.

though it is technically incorrect. Here's how an azimuth and a bearing differ:

An *azimuth* is an angle measured clockwise from north (either true, grid, or magnetic) to your objective. Its value will lie between 0 and 360 degrees. What is called a "bearing" in this book is, strictly speaking, an azimuth.

Bearing is a nautical term that relates the degree reading east or west of a north–south reference line. A bearing compass is divided into four quadrants of 90 degrees (each graduated 0° to 90°). The standard azimuth compass is graduated 0° to 360°.

Here's a comparison of some azimuths and their equivalent bearings:

FIGURE 4-5

Answers to Lost Lake exercise.

Point	True bearing	Distance (miles)	Approximate travel time	Magnetic bearing (to be set on your compass)
A to B	290°	2¾	1½ hours	284°
B to C	341°	1½	¾ hour	335°
C to D	15°	½	20 minutes	9°
D to E	338°	4	2 hours	332°
E to F	274°	3¼	1½ hours	268°
F to G	244°	1⅛	½ hour	238°
G to H	227°	2½	1¼ –1½ hours	221°

H to portage (paddle north up the shoreline to portage): Time—about 15 minutes.

An Azimuth of	Equals a Bearing of
45°	N45°E (north 45 degrees east)
225°	S45°W (south 45 degrees west)
350°	N10°W (north 10 degrees west)

The azimuth/bearing relationship is illustrated in figure 4-6.

Bearings have an advantage when you compute reciprocal (back) directions. Example: The back azimuth of 45° is 225° (45° + 180°). But the back bearing of N45°E is simply S45°W. Figure 4-6 shows the relationship.

FIGURE 4-6

Azimuth/bearing relationship.

The term azimuth is largely unknown outside of professional circles. Most people say bearing when what they really mean is azimuth.

Aiming Off

Proceeding from attack point to attack point is as useful on land as it is on water, with one exception: Trees! Getting around them necessarily means reestablishing your bearing after every run in—not impossible, but awkward enough to preclude pinpoint targeting of your objective. For this reason, precise compass bearings are usually modified by aiming off. This simple procedure ensures you'll hit your objective head-on. Consider the following scenario:

You've parked your car at the road junction at A and have walked the trail to Tarrison Lakes (B). To return, you can follow the winding trail back—three and one-half miles (see the bar scale below) or, you can

FIGURE 4-7

Aiming off map.

Declination = 10° East

Countour Interval = 50 feet

Scale 1:50,000

Miles 1   0   1   2   3

eliminate more than a mile by heading cross country to A. However, if you compute a direct compass bearing from B to A, your chance of hitting A is extremely small. It's doubtful you can maintain a precise compass course over this rough and wooded ground. Better to compensate for your wandering by aiming off to the southwest, say to an imaginary point (D) on the road. If you set your compass for 240° (for simplicity, assume the declination is zero—see Declination section below) you will strike the road somewhere near point D. Makes no difference whether you are north or south of D. Once on the road just follow it south to your starting point. Simple, isn't it?

Wouldn't it be shorter to hike due west to the road, towards point C? Shorter, yes. Easier, no! The contour lines (50 foot contouir interval) suggest you'll be puffing up hills and sliding down valleys. The B to D plan is much more level.

If aiming off is useful on land, it's even more useful on water. For example: Suppose you're located at point G on the Lost Lake map (figure 4-2). You want to take the portage trail that leads to the South Arm of Maze Lake, just north of H. There are three portages leading out of Bay 3, but only one goes to South Arm. From G to the South Arm trail is about 3 miles. A 4-degree error over this distance would cause you to miss your objective by at least 1,100 feet (remember, 1 degree of compass error equals 92 feet per mile of ground error), or nearly a quarter mile—enough to send you scurrying down the wrong trail.

The solution is to aim off to H—an unidentifiable point just south of the trail. Then, when you reach the shoreline, turn right (north). The first path you come to is the correct one.

Declination

A compass points (actually, it doesn't point—it lines up with the Earth's magnetic field) to magnetic north, not true north. This angular difference, called declination, must be considered whenever you use your compass (figures 4-8 and 4-9). In the eastern United States the declination is westerly; in the western United States it's easterly. If you live right on the imaginary line that goes directly through both the true and magnetic north poles (called the agonic line), your declination will be zero.

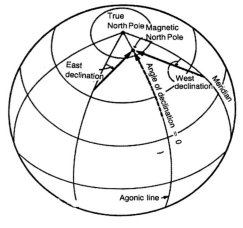

On the other hand, if you live east or west of the agonic line, your compass will be in error, since the true north pole is not in the same place as the magnetic north pole. As you can see from the declination chart, the farther away you are from the agonic line, the greater the declination. Moreover, the magnetic pole is constantly moving; because of this, declination will vary from year to year as well as place to place. Consequently, it's not possible for compass makers to factory adjust a compass to account for this variation.

FIGURE 4-8

Global declination chart.

To find the exact declination for your area, consult your topo-

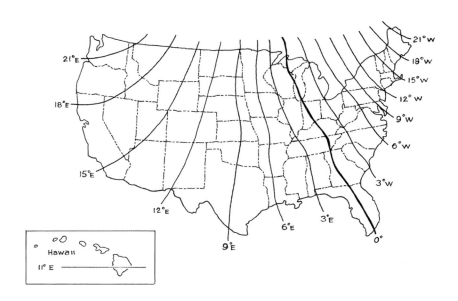

FIGURE 4-9

Standard declination chart. Values are representative, not precise.

graphic map. You'll find the declination value in a diagram in the lower map margin. It will look something like what is shown in figure 4-10.

Note that the "legs" of the declination diagram in figure 4-10 are not drawn to angular scale (some diagrams are). The angles are slightly exaggerated for clarity—a note to that effect appears in the legend. Consequently, you shouldn't use the direction of the magnetic flag as an accurate pointing for your compass. Instead, adjust the instrument mathematically, as explained in the following section.

FIGURE 4-10

Declination value diagram. Use diagram only to obtain numerical values

APPROXIMATE MEAN DECLINATION
1962 FOR
CENTER MAP
Annual change decreasing 6.3'

1. The star (★) indicates the direction of true north. This leg of the diagram runs parallel to a line of longitude.

2. The flag (▶) points to magnetic north. If the flag is to the right (east) of the north star, the area declination is east. If it's to the left of the star, the declination is west.

3. The black sphere (●) indicates the direction of the grid lines on the map. (Some maps use a small letter y instead of a sphere.) Remember: Topographic maps do not have lines of longitude imprinted on their faces, but they do have grid lines. The two are not the same! When you peel the skin off a globe (Earth) and lay it flat, you distort the curved meridians. This distortion—or variation from true north—is reported in all declination diagrams.

Interpreting the Diagram

In figure 4-10, grid north is 13 minutes west of true north. Disregard the 4 mils number. That's for military use. (The military compass is graduated in "mils." There are 6,400 mils in a circle. North is zero mils, east is 1,600 mils, south is 3,200 mils, etc. Mils are further subdivided into tenths and hundredths. Minutes and seconds are not used.)

Magnetic north is 31°24' (31°37' - 0°13') east of true north (you should round it off to 31 degrees). This is the direction your compass needle will point. It is also the value of the *declination*, defined as the angle between true north and magnetic north.

You can also determine *grid declination* from the diagram. It is the angle between *grid north* and magnetic north—in this case, 31°37' east, or 32 degrees when rounded off. The section on grid declination on page 51 tells you how to use this important figure.

To Determine Declination without a Map

If you have a GPS receiver, you can access the declination of your location through the setup menu in the instrument. Most GPS units round off the declination value to the nearest whole number, which is plenty accurate for compass navigation.

The following Web sites provide precise (to the nearest minute of arc) declination and latitude/longitude values for any place in the world:

• In the United States: www.ngdc.noaa.gov/seg/geomag/jsp/struts/calc Declination

• In Canada: http://gsc.nrcan.gc.ca/geomag/field/mdcalc_e.php

Dealing with Declination

Check out the declination on the Lost Lake map (figure 4-2). It equals 6 degrees east. There are no grid lines on this map, hence, no need to identify grid north.

As stated, maps are almost always drawn in their true perspective (any variation here is so small it can be ignored). So any bearing you determine *from the map* by using the top of the map or the east or west border (line of longitude) as a north reference, is, by definition, a *true* bearing. The bearings you computed in the A-through-H point-to-point exercise were therefore all true bearings. *Now you must change these true values to magnetic ones that will be set on your compass* and fol-lowed on the ground—easy enough, if you remember the simple rhyme:

Note:

It makes no difference in which direction (north, south, east, or west, or something in between) you are going on the map sheet. If the declination is east, you always subtract its value from your true map bearing. If it's west, you add it. If this is confusing, you may want to buy a compass that can be adjusted for declination.

Declination east—compass least

(Subtract east declination from your map direction.)

Declination west—compass best

(Add west declination to your map direction.)

Your true bearing from A to B in the Lost Lake exercise was 290 degrees. Change it to a magnetic bearing by application of the rhyme. Subtract 6 degrees and you get 284. Adjust your compass for this new heading and take off. You'll hit point B head-on.

Conversely, if the declination were west, you would add its value (290 + 6 = 296) to your compass reading.

Okay, test time . . . again. Convert all your *true* Lost Lake bearings to *magnetic* ones. Answers are found in figure 4-5.

Grid Declination

Grid lines take the guesswork out of aligning your protractor or orienteering compass to map north. Remember, however, that grid lines don't point *true north*, so you'll have to compensate for their variation.

Any bearing you compute off a map using grid north (any grid line) as the north reference line is, by definition, a *grid bearing*. Before you can follow this bearing on the ground, you must first convert it to a *magnetic bearing* by application of the "east is least, west is best" rhyme.

The grid declination in figure 4-10 is 31°37' east, or 32 degrees, when rounded off. Subtract 32 degrees from your grid bearing and set this value on your compass. That's all there is to it. The procedure is identical to that used to change a true bearing to a magnetic one.

In truth, we're splitting hairs here, for grid north is so close to true north (just 13 minutes away) that the difference is meaningless. This isn't always the case, however, so check out the values before you commit to your *accurate* field bearings. Admittedly, true and grid north seldom vary by much more than 3 degrees, so for typical field use the two can usually be considered as one.

Tape Method of Adjusting the Compass for Declination

If you don't want to mess with the mechanics of adding or subtracting declination values from your true or grid bearings, you can adjust your compass to compensate. Here's how.

Given: You have computed a *true* map bearing of 60 degrees to your objective. The area declination is 10 degrees east.

Procedure: Place a narrow piece of tape across the face of the compass housing so that it goes over the needle pivot and intersects both the 10-degree and 190-degree marks. Your compass is now adjusted to compensate for a 10-degree east declination.

Now . . . hold the compass in front of you and find the bearing on the ground—only *don't* frame the magnetic needle in the doghouse (printed arrow in the capsule) as is customary. Instead, align it with the tape mark, which is 10 degrees east of north. Note that you are actually facing a bearing of 50 (60 degrees minus 10 degrees).

Conversely, if the declination were 10 degrees west, you would apply the tape so that it intersected the 350-degree (that's 10 degrees west) and 170-degree marks. As you might guess, the mechanical declination adjustments on sophisticated compasses use this very procedure.

Adjusting Your Map for Declination

You can also adjust your map for declination by drawing lines across its face that run parallel to the north magnetic pole. Then, when you compute map headings, just align the printed arrow in the capsule of your orienteering compass with these lines rather than "map north" (top of the map). All competitive orienteering maps are set up like this. However, the system works much better with small orienteering maps than with 2½-foot-square topos. Try drawing parallel lines across a standard-size topographic map and you'll see why. Best stick with a more conventional treatment of declination.

Updating the Declination

The magnetic poles are constantly moving. Their location changes from year to year (and from minute to minute). Movements are subtle, however—generally small enough that only surveyors interested in extreme accuracy need worry about them.

The problem only surfaces when you're working off a very old map. For example, the legend in figure 4-10 states "APPROXIMATE MEAN DECLINATION 1962 . . . annual change decreasing 6.3'."

This means that magnetic north (the flag) is moving *westward* (decreasing) by 6.3 minutes per year. Updating the declination to 2008 is easy:

1. Determine the elapsed years (2008-1962=46 years).
2. Multiply the annual change by the elapsed years (6.3 x 46 years)= 289.8 minutes.
3. Convert minutes to whole degrees (289.8 ÷ 60=4.8 . . . or 5 degrees).
4. Subtract this figure from the 1962 declination of 32 degrees (32° - 5° =27°). Your declination for 2008 is 27 degrees east.

If this seems like too much work, just read the current declination value from your GPS unit or log on to one of the declination Web sites suggested on page 50.

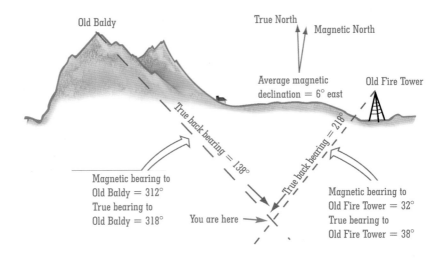

Old Baldy

True North

Magnetic North

Average magnetic
declination = 6° east

Old Fire Tower

True back bearing = 138°

True back bearing = 218°

Magnetic bearing to
Old Baldy = 312°
True bearing to
Old Baldy = 318°

You are here →

Magnetic bearing to
Old Fire Tower = 32°
True bearing to
Old Fire Tower = 38°

FIGURE 4-11

Position of triangulation.

Position by Triangulation

Suppose you're lost on a large, mazelike lake, but you can recognize two or more topographical features off in the distance. Use your orienteering compass (or protractor and conventional compass) to find your position by *triangulation*.

Pick out one point on the horizon that you can identify—Old Baldy, in this case (see figure 4-11). Shoot a magnetic bearing to the point (bearing = 312 degrees). Change this magnetic bearing to a true bearing by reverse application of the rhyme: 312°+ 6°=318°. Draw the back (reciprocal) bearing (318°–180°=138°) through Old Baldy, using your compass baseplate and a sharp pencil.

Now . . . using the baseplate as a straight edge, draw your line. Repeat the exercise using another point that you can identify (the old fire tower). You are located where the two lines cross.

Okay, now for another test, again using the Lost Lake map in figure 4-2. You can identify Dunker Hill at a magnetic bearing of 253 degrees and Kaby Lookout at a magnetic bearing of 4 degrees. Where are you located? **Clue:** Don't forget to apply the declination. You'll find the answer on the next page.

Relocating a Good Fishing Spot by Triangulation

You don't need to identify points on a map to use triangulation. In fact, you don't need a map at all. Suppose you've discovered a real hot spot—the fish are biting like crazy. You definitely want to come here again. Problem is, there are no identifying landmarks to guide the way. And the fishing hole is small, just a dozen yards in diameter. How on Earth will you find this place again?

Easy! Just shoot compass bearings to two or more places on the shoreline. The tall pine on the right (figure 4-12) and broken-down

FIGURE 4-12

Relocating a good fishing spot by triangulation.

cabin at left are ideal. But your points need not be so sophisticated. A moss-covered boulder or leaning tree will do. Anything that won't run off will work. Since you don't have a map, there's no need to compute back bearings or to draw intersecting lines. Instead, simply record the numbers in a notebook for future reference. Next time you come here, look for the cabin and pine tree. Then position yourself where the two bearings match.

Free Triangulation

This is the same as two-point triangulation, except you need just one reference line. Assume you're hiking along the railroad track in figure 4-13 and want to establish your exact position. In the distance you see a large hill that stands out boldly among the flatlands. You shoot a compass bearing to the hill and get 156 degrees.

Convert this *magnetic* reading to true direction by reverse application of the rhyme: 156° + 10° = 166°. Next, determine the back bearing (166° + 180° = 346°) and plot it on the map. You're located where the line crosses the track.

Use free triangulation any place you can establish a single line of reference—a road, trail, river, creek, lakeshore, or power line.

Answer to triangulation problem: You are located at the north end of Horseshoe Island.

FIGURE 4-13

Free triangulation diagram.

Declination = 10° East

CHAPTER 5

Tricks of the Trade

If you've progressed this far, you're just short of being expert with map and compass. You can now compute map bearings, convert them to magnetic readings, and chart a course through tangled brush or the maze of islands on a fog-bound lake. You know all about aiming off, triangulation, and declination plus a wealth of other navigation procedures.

So congratulations on your hard-earned confidence. You're almost ready to cope with the worst of times on the best of terms. What you need now is practice, practice, practice . . . plus a working knowledge of some tricks of the trade. Here are a few.

Navigation at Night

Over the years I've done a fair amount of black night canoe travel on large sprawling lakes. Most memorable was the time I camped in the Boundary Waters Canoe Area of Minnesota and was awakened to find three bears merrily munching dehydrated prunes that my teen group had carelessly thrown about. We blew whistles, clanged pans, and yelled loudly. No luck. The bruins remained oblivious to the racket and kept right on eating.

When they knocked down one tent, we decided it was time to leave. Within minutes we struck camp and put to sea. There was no moon or stars; just full cloud cover and vast nothingness. Visibility was a flat zero.

Fortunately, I had a flashlight and my Silva Ranger compass. I carefully plotted a beeline for a distant island that had a campsite. Then I set the compass on the floor of my canoe and unerringly kept the luminous point on the magnetic needle aligned with the glowing aid dots that flanked it.

Before we dipped paddles, I carefully computed the distance from our location to the island. It was almost exactly 3 miles. At an approximate paddling speed of 2 cautious miles per hour, we should arrive on target in ninety minutes. I set my watch alarm and peeled out into the blackness of the night.

Exactly eighty minutes later, we touched shore. There was the island . . . and the welcome campsite.

Moral: You need more than good bearings for black night travel. You also need to keep track of your distance and time!

Traveling overland on a dead dark night is another matter. Some years ago, as a forester with the Bureau of Land Management in Oregon, I was lost for three days in the mountains south of Coos Bay. Again, I had my trusty Silva, but this time, no map. Referencing was a matter of the mind: I knew Highway 101 was about 60 miles due west. I tried to travel the first night, but it was no use. After a number of life-threatening falls, I gave up in disgust and waited till sunrise.

Around noon of the third day, I struck a logging road and the sound of a clanging diesel tractor. Humility? You bet. When I returned to work the next day, I never told a soul. After all . . . foresters don't get lost!

Outdoor books are rich with tales of men who traveled the haunting wilds with only the stars or a simple compass to guide them. Of course, it can be done and has been done, but the risks of injury are very real.

However, night travel takes on new dimensions if the sky is gentle gray or if you have a full moon or powerful headlamp to guide the way. But don't rely on luminous compass points to keep you on track. Compass "night sights" are very primitive: Without frequent light to recharge their chemical batteries, they fail. None will last the night. A flashlight—or other light source—is essential.

As to navigation by the stars, I know of no one who has ever had to resort to such folly. If you are lost or without a compass, you have no business traveling at night, and if you do have a compass you certainly don't need the stars. Moreover, trees and topographical features sometimes prevent you from keeping the North Star in view. Such star navigation makes interesting reading, but it's impractical. However, if you're interested in this sort of thing, check out a Boy Scout handbook or a standard text on surveying.

River Navigation

Everything in this book has been necessarily centered around land and lake navigation. After all, that's where you'll be navigating most of the time. But suppose you want to canoe or raft a wild, brawny river. Are there navigational concerns other than those mentioned in chapter 2?

You bet! With the impact of man on river systems, it is becoming more and more important for river users to know what the water conditions are before they go afloat. Many local and even far northern rivers are now dam controlled and are very dangerous at high water or impossible to paddle during the "walking levels" of late summer. Barbed-wire fences strung across rivers maim and kill boaters each year, and the people who string these fences usually have the law on their side. Each year, we read about canoeists and fishermen who inadvertently paddled over a dam because they didn't know it was there.

If you boat rivers, you must be able to accurately locate and identify dams, rapids, fences, and other obstacles that can endanger your trip. The symbols for many of these appear on your topographic map, but not all. Frequently what's there is incorrect. Here are some ways to outfox the inadequacies of your map.

1. Continually check the *level* of the tree line as you paddle along. If tree heights fall off suddenly, there's a dam or falls ahead.

2. Maps do not indicate obstacles that are the result of river turbulence. Waves pile up on the outside of bends, and so does debris. Except in very low water, you should always stay on the *inside* curves of a river.

3. It is very difficult to fix your position on a river. A compass will be useful for rough directions only. Of course, you can reaffirm your location at major bends, rapids, or incoming streams, or you may be fortunate enough to locate an identifiable object upon which you can plot a line of free triangulation.

Lastly, some of the best sources of river conditions are the people who live in the area. Always check with them before embarking on a river, even if you've run it many times. Be aware, however, that locals tend to exaggerate the dangers of their river. So especially seek out foresters or professional people who work in the area. Outdoors people will generally tell it like it is . . . or at least they'll exaggerate less.

And if one day your dreams take you to the far north, where rivers run cold and help is an airplane ride away, you'll need to know (*absolutely know!*) your precise location at all times. Contrary to what you may have read or heard, compasses are generally quite reliable near the Arctic Circle—that is, if you can correctly apply the declination—which may change with each few miles you travel!

Navigating Streams and Moose Trails

Finding your way through a maze of beaver streams and moose trails calls for resourcefulness. Remember, modern maps are made from aerial photos, and if you can't see the sky because of a dense tree canopy or tall grass, the plane-mounted camera can't necessarily see the stream. Therefore, your map may be in error in these places, though the general flow of the watercourse—minus the switchbacks—is usually accurate.

The heads and mouths of small streams are almost always plotted correctly, but deciphering the maze in between often calls for a ready compass. Moreover, streambeds are constantly changing, and these changes will not be reflected on a topographic map that is many years old.

Some hints for navigating small meandering streams: 1) Where a stream forks, take the route with the strongest flow, even if it looks more restrictive than a broader channel. If there is no discernible current, note which way the grass bends in the channel and follow. 2) Check your compass frequently—don't rely on your map, especially if it is many years old. 3) If you come to a dead end and see a portage trail, scout it before you carry your canoe or boat across. Your "portage" may simply be a heavily used animal trail that leads to a connecting tributary or a dead-end pond.

Your Watch as a Compass

Although of questionable accuracy, direction finding using a watch is at times convenient when you want a rough, quick direction but you don't want to get out your compass. If your watch is correctly set for the

FIGURE 5-1

Using a watch as a compass.

time zone in which you're traveling, just hold the watch horizontal and point the hour hand at the sun. Halfway between the hour hand and twelve o'clock is south (see figure 5-1). Such showmanship will impress your friends when things get dull on a long trip.

By the way, you can also use your compass as a watch. Just keep in mind the hourly positions of the sun, which are:

6:00 a.m.—*east*   3:00 p.m.—*southwest*

9:00 a.m.—*southeast*   6:00 p.m.—*west*

noon—*south*

Using the Stars as a Compass

Follow the two "pointer" stars on the cup of the Big Dipper to the North Star (Polaris), which is the tail star of the Little Dipper (figure 5-2). The Dippers are circumpolar constellations, so they're visible year-round

FIGURE 5-2

How to determine north by using the stars.

from any place in the Northern Hemisphere. Polaris is seldom more than 1 degree east or west of true north.

To Determine Declination by the Stars

If your map does not provide magnetic declination information—and you don't have a GPS receiver or a computer online—drive two pointed sticks into the ground and line them up with the North Star, as illustrated in figure 5-3. The longer stick should be north of the shorter stick. The angle between the compass needle and true north is the magnetic declination of your area. Be sure to note whether the declination is east or west! This procedure works best when declination angles are very large.

FIGURE 5-3

Field method of determining declination.

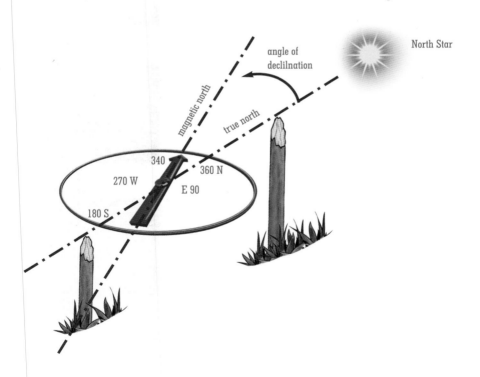

Baselines

Most every book on wilderness navigation has a chapter devoted to helping "the lost hunter"—relocating your remote camp, finding the remains of the deer you shot, etc. But it's all simply a matter of baselines; that is, you establish a reliable handrail (road, stream, power line, etc.). Then use it as a reference line for your bearings. Figure 1-1 is a typical example of this relationship—one that again proves the importance of a map. Note, however, that you don't need a formal map to travel the backwoods with confidence. A mind relationship is often enough. My three-day "confusion" in the Oregon woods is a case in point. I knew Highway 101 was due west. And that was sufficient!

As you can see, there's no substitute for common sense. To this add a good map and a compass and a practiced hand, and you'll have all the tools you need to confidently navigate the backcountry.

The Global Positioning System (GPS)

GPS (global positioning system) receivers are hot new navigational aids. Twenty-four satellites that orbit Earth twice a day transmit precise time (via an atomic clock) and positioning information. With a GPS receiver you can determine your location on Earth to within 10 meters or less in a matter of minutes or seconds. Or you can enter a set of coordinates of a place you want to go, and the GPS receiver will provide a compass bearing and distance that will be updated by satellite information as you walk, drive, fly, or paddle. Press a button and you get a speed readout and an estimated time of arrival.

Even without a map, a GPS is extremely useful. Enter your starting position and save it as a waypoint. Establish other waypoints as you proceed—then, like Hansel and Gretel, follow your electronic bread crumbs home.

Most of today's GPS receivers are "menu driven," which somewhat simplifies operation. Nonetheless, mastery of the instrument requires considerable study plus a working knowledge of maps and navigational procedures. All hand-held GPS units operate on small batteries, which could fail when you need them most. For this reason, it's impractical to leave the instrument on for continuous positioning. The most useful GPS feature is its ability to verify your location on a map.

Maps must have some sort of reference system to which your GPS can relate. United States and Canadian topo-

GPS receivers are hot new navigational aids. The reading on the author's GPS (66°30.093') indicates that he is about to cross the Arctic Circle, which, in 2000, is defined as 66° 33' 39" N latitude.

graphic maps are marked with degrees of latitude and longitude. Canadian topographic maps and U.S. military maps also use the Universal Transverse Mercator (UTM) system that is simpler because it's decimal-based. Any GPS unit can be set to read Lat/Lon or UTM coordinates, as you prefer. Some maps made by private companies for use in specialized areas, such as national parks and wilderness areas, don't have either UTM or Lat/Lon markings, which means you can't use GPS with them.

The author uses his GPS to check his location on a topographic map. Along the Snake River, Yukon Territories, Canada. Note waterproof case for the map and GPS.

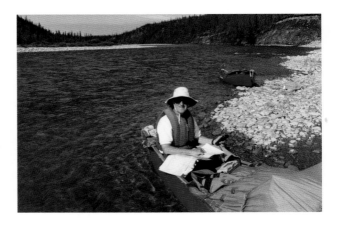

A GPS receiver will not replace your map and compass, but it will add to the fun—and safety—of exploring wild places.

Using A GPS Receiver With Your Map

If you have tried to plot a GPS position on a map to the nearest 100 meters using degrees, minutes, and seconds of latitude/longitude, you know it isn't easy. That's because latitude/longitude is not a rectangular grid—the distance between longitude lines varies as you go north or south. To interpolate fractions of degrees, you must use a latitude/longitude "roamer" (a plastic template scale) like the one shown in figure 6-1. It would be far easier to plot a precise fix if the grid lines were rectangular (that is, if there was no convergence).

Enter the Universal Transverse Mercator grid. It is perfectly rectangular, and coordinate values are in meters. UTM coordinates are referenced or overprinted on all U.S. and Canadian topographic maps. Every GPS unit can be set to read them.

FIGURE 6-1:

A latitude/longitude roamer (scale template) is essential to accurately plot latitude/longitude points on a topographic map. UTM locations can be accurately eyeballed.

What Is UTM?

UTM divides the world into sixty zones (figure 6-2). Each zone spans 6 degrees of longitude and 164 degrees of latitude (it covers from latitude 80° south to latitude 84° north). Zones 10 through 19 cover most of the United States and Canada. Lettered bands of latitude divide the zones (figure 6-3). A central meridian runs through the middle of each zone and is assigned an arbitrary (false) easting value of 500,000 meters to avoid using negative numbers. Thus, the grid values to the west of each central meridian have an easting value of less than 500,000

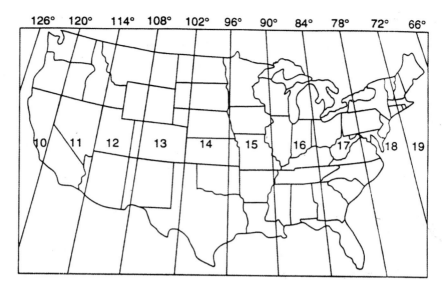

FIGURE 6-2

UTM divides the world into 60 zones. Zones 10–19 cover most of the U.S. and Canada.

meters; those to the east of each central meridian have an "easting" value greater than 500,000 meters.

To specify a point in the North Hemisphere you give its distance in meters from the false east origin (easting), and the equator (northing). Points south of the equator are handled differently: In order to have northing values increase going from south to north (and to avoid negative numbers), the equator is given a false northing value of 10,000,000 meters.

Sound complicated? Don't fret. All this is overly academic. To use your GPS receiver with UTM coordinates you simply need to know the *hemisphere* and *zone in which you are traveling*, the horizontal *map datum*, and *how to read the coordinates.*

Zone Numbers

You'll find the zone number in the margin of every topographic map. It is expressed as a number (for example, 16) on U.S. topographic maps and as a number, followed by a row letter, on U.S. military maps and Canadian topographic maps. For example, the map section shown in figure 6-4 is in zone 16U, which is in Ontario, Canada (see figure 6-3). If

FIGURE 6-3

Lettered bands of latitude divide the zones. The map section in figure 6-4 is in zone 16U.

you use map coordinates to initialize your GPS or to program a way-point, you'll have to specify the *zone number* and *hemisphere* (northern or southern). Some GPS units allow you to set the complete zone designation (for example, 16U).

Map Datum

A datum is part of a shape that best fits the part of the world that's indicated on your map. The Earth is not a uniform ball, so certain datum systems provide a truer picture than others for some portions of the Earth's surface. Essentially, the map datum tells your GPS what "Earth shape" the map is using. The datum is printed on the bottom of all topographic maps. The three most popular datums are: NAD 27 (North American datum, 1927), WGS 84 (World Geodetic System, 1984), and NAD 83 (North American datum, 1983). There are hundreds of datums—if you use the wrong one, your GPS unit won't provide an

FIGURE 6-4

Can you determine the UTM coordinates of these points?

There's a difference between having a GPS and knowing how to use it. Give yourself time to become familiar with it and learn to use it correctly.

accurate fix. If you set up your GPS receiver to use latitude/longitude, a datum error may result in a map error of as much as 200 meters in North America. But a datum error with UTM coordinates is more serious—up to 300 meters in North America.

When you enter a waypoint, your GPS receiver puts that waypoint into memory under the WGS 84 datum (its default datum), after first converting it from the datum you have currently chosen. If you later choose a different datum, your GPS will translate the coordinates and display them in the new datum you select.

Reading the Coordinates

Figure 6-5 illustrates how to read the coordinates. The grid value (easting) of line A-A would be reported as 357,000 meters east (A-A is actually 143,000 meters west of its central meridian). Line B-B is 4,276,000 meters north of the equator. Point P is 800 meters east of line A-A and 750 meters north of line B-B.

Thus, the UTM designation of point P (to the nearest meter) is 357800E / 4276750N. (Note that a "complete" UTM designation would include the zone number.) If there is an odd number of a digit it's because the preceding zero in the easting value has been dropped.

The zero will appear on the display of your GPS receiver. Some GPS units will also display the complete zone designation (for example, 15T). The rule is to "read right up," which means you should read the easting value first and the northing value second. Strangely, some GPS units list the northing value first.

See if you can determine the UTM coordinates of points a, b, and c on the map in figure 6-4. Eyeball them—don't use a metric ruler or a coordinate roamer; you probably won't have one when you're hiking. Note that the first easting digit and the first two northing digits on the map are smaller than those that follow. These "secondary" numbers represent hundreds of thousands and millions of meters, so they are reduced in size to eliminate confusion. The downsized numbers will automatically show up on your GPS.

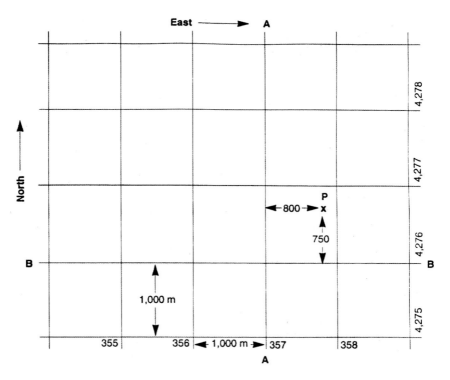

FIGURE 6-5

Reading the coordinates. (Courtesy USGS, fact sheet 142-97)

Answers:

a: 332300E / 5849500N or 0332300E / 5849500N

b: 332400E / 5848800N or 0332400E / 5848800N

c: 333800E / 5848300N or 0333800E / 5848300N

The beauty of the UTM system is that you get a fairly accurate fix by plotting just three numbers. Consider the position of point a: The boldfaced numbers 323/495 (03**323**00 / 58**495**00) indicate that you are three-tenths (0.3) of a grid square east of line 32 and five-tenths (0.5) of a grid square north of line 49.

Say you've been hiking for an hour and want to know your location. Just turn on your GPS unit and plot the three important easting and northing numbers on your map. Then turn off the GPS to save batteries.

A military map note: Secondary numbers are omitted on military maps. The Military Grid Reference System (MGRS), a slight modification of UTM, drops the small digits and uses a two-letter identifier to indicate the 100,000-meter square of operation.

A Checklist for Setting Up Your GPS Unit

Initialize your GPS unit according to instructions. In the setup menu:

1. Define the coordinate system (UTM or latitude/longitude). I prefer UTM.

2. Select the correct horizontal datum for the map you are using.

3. Select which "north" (true or magnetic) your receiver will use as a reference. I prefer true north because GPS bearings (to waypoints) are in true map perspective. However, if you are confused by declination, select magnetic north. Then you can set the bearings to waypoints that your GPS computes directly on your hand compass without messing with math.

4. Set your GPS to read the same units (feet or meters) as your map.

Reminder: Be sure you have programmed into your GPS unit the hemisphere and zone number (or complete number-and-letter zone designation) in which you are traveling.

GPS Tips and Concerns

1. Don't take GPS *elevation* readings as gospel. The Earth blocks enough important satellites to prevent accurate readings. Elevations can be off by dozens of feet! If you want accurate elevations, use a calibrated barometer or the contour lines on your map.

2. Your GPS will convert UTM coordinates to latitude/longitude and vice versa. Simply change the coordinate system in the setup menu. You can avoid serious number errors when programming UTM coordinates if, after you've programmed the coordinates, you switch to latitude/longitude mode and "eyeball" plot their locations on your map. If the latitude/longitude of your waypoint is roughly correct, your UTM coordinates are probably correct too. If not, you've made a serious UTM number error.

    If you have a computer online, you can use the UTM Converter at www.cellspark.com/utmconverter.html to convert UTM values to latitude/longitude and vice versa.

3. If you want to share UTM coordinate information with someone, be sure you reference your eastings and northings to the map sheet you are using. Technically, you should provide the horizontal datum, complete grid-zone designation, and the full easting and northing.

    Example: Nad 27 /16U / 332,300E / 5,849,500N

4. For precision plotting, you'll want an inexpensive plastic coordinate scale, like the one in figure 6-1 (from GPS Scales/Waypoint Enterprises; see appendix 4). Some orienteering-style compasses have UTM coordinate scales—but not latitude/longitude scales printed on the baseplate.

Some Things to Consider When Choosing a GPS Receiver

1. Learning how to use a GPS unit is like mastering a computer; if you don't use it, you'll lose it! The best plan is to buy a unit that will

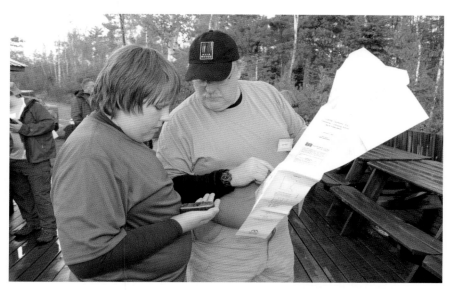

A basic GPS and an accurate map help plot a safe and enjoyable course for two outdoors enthusiasts.

mount in your car. Get a dashboard mount and cigarette-lighter plug so you can practice setting waypoints, save track data, and master other operations without running down batteries. You won't become proficient if you use your GPS just a few times a year.

2. Large GPS units are generally more user friendly than small ones. Miniature GPS receivers often have awkwardly placed controls, and their tiny antennas don't access satellites as fast or reliably as bigger antennas.

3. Not all "waterproof" GPS units have waterproof battery compartments!

4. Every GPS receiver should have a simulator mode so you can learn the intricacies of operation more quickly.

5. Be aware that alkaline batteries don't work in subzero weather. If you'll be out in the cold, choose lithium batteries instead. Lithiums have a longer shelf life too.

6. Be sure that the position numbers (latitude-longitude or UTM) are large enough to read in dim light.

Things you don't need in a GPS:

- *Electronic compass.* It must be recalibrated when you change batteries or move out of its calibration range. If the battery fails, your compass does too.
- *Barometer:* A barometer must be frequently recalibrated to provide accurate air pressure readings and elevations. Yes, you will get a relative read-out without calibration, which is useful to determine weather trends.
- *Thermometer:* Electronic thermometers are slow to register readings. They're one more thing to drain battery power.
- *Color:* Color is nice but it consumes battery power and it doesn't add accuracy or utility.

Recommended Reading

For more information on GPS, I suggest the following:

GPS Land Navigation, by Michael Ferguson (Glassford Publishing, 1997). This is by far the best book on GPS navigation.

U.S. Geological Survey Fact Sheet 142-97. Available from the USGS; see chapter 2 for contact information.

Appendix 1
Common U.S. Map Symbols

Topographic Map Symbols			
Primary highway		Gravel beach or glacial moraine	
Secondary highway		Woods (green)	
Light-duty road		Scrub (green)	
Unimproved road		Orchard (green)	
Trail		Rock bare or awash	
Bridge		Group of rocks bare or awash	
Building: small; large		Sunken rock	
Cemetery: small; large		Intermittent stream	
Standard gauge single track; station		Disappearing stream	
Abandoned track		Large falls, rapids	
Power transmission line; pole; tower		Masonry dam	
Telephone or telegraph line		Intermittent lake or pond	
Quarry or open pit mine		Dry lake	
Mine tunnel or cave entrance		Water well; spring or seep	
Sand or mud area, dunes or shifting sand		Marsh or swamp	

Appendix 2
Common Terms

Agonic line: A line or zero declination. At any point along this imaginary line, the compass will point true north.

Aiming off: The navigator aims to the right or left of his objective, rather than straight at it. This creates a purposeful error in a known direction, which helps in targeting the objective.

Attack point: A point on the map that is easy to identify on land (hilltop, road junction, railroad crossing, etc.). Same as a "check point."

Azimuth: An angle measured clockwise from north (true, grid, or magnetic) to your objective.

Back bearing: Also called reciprocal bearing. It is the opposite direction from which you came. Or 180 degrees plus or minus your forward bearing.

Baseline: A handrail that's used as a reference line for positioning when afield. The navigator works on one side or the other of the baseline. A return bearing is plotted to the baseline, which is then followed "home."

Baseplate: The ruled plastic base of an orienteering compass.

Bearing: A direction, in degrees, from where you are to where you want to go. Technically, the degree reading east or west of a north-south reference line.

Cardinal points: The primary directions—north, east, south, west.

Compass rose: The 360 degrees of the compass circle.

Contour interval: The difference in elevation (usually above sea level) from one contour line to another.

Contour lines: Light brown lines on a map that indicate height above sea level.

Declination: The direction in which the compass needle points. More accurately, it's the angular difference between true north and magnetic north, or between grid north and magnetic north (called "grid declination"). Expressed in degrees east or west of the agonic line.

Declination diagram: A diagram in the legend of topographic maps that gives the value of the area declination.

Direction-of-travel arrow: An arrow inscribed on the plastic base plate of orienteering compasses points toward your objective when the compass is properly oriented (needle centered in the doghouse).

Doghouse: A slang term for the printed arrow inside the housing of orienteering compasses. When the "dog" is in the "house" (magnetic needle inside printed arrow of housing), the compass is properly oriented.

GPS (global positioning system) receiver: An electronic unit that receives positioning information off orbiting satellites. With a civilian GPS model, you can locate your position anywhere on Earth in a matter of minutes. Accuracy is 10 meters or less.

Grid lines: Interconnecting lines superimposed over the face of topographic maps.

Grid north: The direction the grid lines point with respect to true north.

Handrail: A topographic feature that you can follow to your objective, such as a road, river, creek, power line, trail, or lakeshore.

Housing: The part of the compass that contains the magnetic needle.

Index: A master map that contains information for ordering topographical maps. Also the place on a compass where the bearing is read.

Intercardinal points: Intermediate compass points—northeast, southeast, southwest, northwest.

Latitude: The distance in degrees north or south of the equator.

Longitude: The distance in degrees east or west of the prime meridian located at Greenwich, England.

Magnetic north: The direction the compass needle points.

Map aid lines: Parallel lines inside the housing of orienteering compasses. When these are aligned to map north, the compass will give a proper bearing you can follow on the ground.

Meridians: Same as lines of longitude. Meridians run true north and south.

North: There are three norths—true (geographic), magnetic (direction the compass needle points), and grid (direction the grid lines run).

Orienteering: Competitive sport combining cross-country running and compass directions to locate specific points (called controls) on the ground.

Parallels: Lines of latitude. These run "parallel" to the equator.

Planimetric map: A map that does not indicate elevation above sea level; Example: a common road map.

Protractor: A plastic arc used for measuring angles.

Scale: The relationship between map and ground distance. Expressed as a representative fraction, such as 1:250,000.

Symbols: Icons on maps that depict primarily man-made features.

Topographic map: A map that shows topography in three dimensions with the aid of contour lines.

USGS (United States Geological Survey): Place where you order topographic maps.

Variation: A nautical term for declination.

Appendix 3
Metric Conversions

Metric	English	Approximation
1 centimeter (cm)	= 0.39 inch	1 inch = about 2.5 cm
1 meter (m)	= 39.4 inches = 3.28 feet = 1.094 yards	Just over a yard
100 meters	= 109 yards	A little longer than a football field
1000 meters	= 1 kilometer (1 km) = 0.62 mile	Just over a half mile When driving in Canada: your speed in miles x 0.6 = kilometers

Appendix 4
Sources of Products

Aloksak waterproof plastic bags
(800) 355–1126

www.watchfuleyedesigns.com or www.Aloksak.com

Waterproof and odorproof zipper-lock bags. Used by government agencies and the military.

Cooke Custom Sewing
(651) 784–8777

www.cookecustomsewing.com

Superior tarps, packs, winter mukluks, and specialized canoeing gear.

Forestry Suppliers, Inc.
(800)647–5368; www.forestry-suppliers.com

All sorts of tools and navigational aids for professional foresters and engineers.

GPS Scales/Waypoint Enterprises
(888) 412–2600 or (928) 537–9163

www.gpsscales.com

Map scales ("roamers") for latitude/longitude and UTM positioning, and videos that teach how to use a GPS unit.

Index

About the Author

Cliff Jacobson is one of North America's most respected outdoors writers and wilderness guides. He is a professional canoe guide and outfitter, a wilderness canoeing and camping consultant, and the author of more than a dozen top-selling books on camping and canoeing. His popular DVD, *The Forgotten Skills*, details the most important campcraft procedures.

Cliff's methods are proven by the sweat of pack and paddle and are reminiscent of the days when skills were more important than things. He is respected by educators for his backcountry ethics, water quality, and wilderness navigation curricula. This book is largely based on the map and compass curriculum he developed for the Minnesota Department of Natural Resources.

In 2003 the American Canoe Association presented Cliff with the Legends of Paddling Award and inducted him into the ACA Hall of Fame.